Mourning Light I

Second Edition

Tracy Reneé Lee, FD, GC-C
Funeral Director, Certified Grief Counselor

For additional books go to

www.QueenCityFuneralHome.com
or
www.MourningCoffee.com

Printed in the United States of America
ISBN – 10:0989444783
ISBN – 13:978098444781

DEDICATION

In memory of
Preston McConkie,
my friend.

FROM THE AUTHOR

I have written Mourning Light to help survivors traverse the treacherous waters of loss and grief. I have written it very simply so that in their delicate state, they may be able to quickly read and understand the information between its pages.

When one has lost a significant loved one, even the simplest of tasks becomes difficult and often seems insurmountable. One's coping skills falter causing insecurities that would not ordinarily exist. This is a natural response to loss, yet many do not know it.

I hope my simple book will help you understand what you will experience on your recovery journey and that it will offer you guidance and comfort through this difficult and painful experience.

It is in no way meant as a substitution for professional counseling.

As you read this book, you will notice there are areas for you to record notes. One of my clients wrote notes in her book as she read it the first time. She found it very comforting and useful as she was able to track her recovery. She suggested that others might benefit from such an exercise, so I have added a place for you to record your thoughts and notes as you travese your road to recovery.

Tracy Renee Lee, FD, GC-C
Queen City Funeral Home

The BRIEFs in this book are meant to help you understand your experience and help give you insights to navigate back to a place in life where you can function more easily.

They are in no way meant as a substitution for professional counseling.

The Grief BRIEFs in this book are available to you as videos at
www.MourningCoffee.com.

If you feel that you cannot concentrate enough to read this material, please go to

www.MourningCoffee.com
and watch the Grief BRIEFs as videos.

CONTENTS

1	Signs & Symptoms:	Forgetting Memories	1
2	Signs & Symptoms:	Ailments of the Soul	2
3	Signs & Symptoms:	Grief or Depression	3
4	Signs & Symptoms:	Sleep Disturbances	4
5	Signs & Symptoms:	Appetite Disturbances	5
6	Signs & Symptoms:	Absentmindedness	6
7	Complication:	Social Withdrawal	7
8	Signs & Symptoms:	Dreams of the Dead	8
9	Complication:	Painful Triggers	9
10	Signs & Symptoms:	Searching	10
11	Signs & Symptoms:	Sighing	11
12	Signs & Symptoms:	Hyperactivity	12
13	Signs & Symptoms:	Tears	13
14	Complication:	Mistaken Grief	14
15	Complication:	Worry	15
16	Expectation:	Mourning Equals Adapting	16
17	Expectation:	Phases of Mourning	17
18	Expectation:	Tasks of Mourning	18
19	Expectation:	Grief Work	19
20	Expectation:	Sadness	20
21	Signs & Symptoms	Numbing of the Senses	21
22	Signs & Symptoms:	Hallucinations	22
23	Signs & Symptoms:	Competitive Behaviors	23
24	Stage of Grief:	Anger	24
25	Complication:	Guilt	25
26	Signs & Symptoms:	Anxiety	26
27	Signs & Symptoms:	Loneliness	27
28	Signs & Symptoms:	Fatigue	28
29	Signs & Symptoms:	Helplessness	29
30	Complication:	Feelings of Emancipation	30
31	Signs & Symptoms:	Shock	31
32	Signs & Symptoms:	Yearning	32

33 Guilt:	Relief	33
34 Recovery Tool:	Share Your Story	34
35 Complication:	Frozen Imperfection	35
36 Recovery Tool:	Exercise	36
37 Recovery Tool:	Religion	37
38 Recovery Tool:	Friends and Family	38
39 Recovery Tool:	Hobbies	39
40 Support:	Psychotherapy	40
41 Support:	Support Group	41
42 Recovery Tool:	Traditions	42
43 Recovery Tool:	Animal Companionship	43
44 Complication:	Breakdown	44
45 Complication:	Delayed Grief	45
46 Recovery Tool:	Developing New Skills	46
47 Complication:	Rebuilding Oneself	47
48 Complication:	Functionality	48
49 Stages:	Accept Reality	49
50 Stages:	Accept Death	50
51 Recovery Tool:	Men and Women Express	51
52 Recovery Tool:	Grief Expressions Recovery	52
53 Recovery Tool:	Patience	53
54 Complication:	Emotional Rollercoaster	54
55 Complication:	Psychological Distress	55
56 Complication:	Stressful Impact	56
57 Complication:	Frequent Ailments	57
58 Complication:	Special Days	58
59 Complication:	Decreased Functionality	59
60 Pre-Occupation:	Forgetfulness	60
61 Pre-Occupation:	Disorganization of Thoughts	61
62 Pre-Occupation:	Difficulties Concentrating	62
63 Pre-Occupation:	Lower Functionality	63
64 Pre-Occupation:	Do Not Drive	64
65 Pre-Occupation:	Lack of Interest	65
66 Signs & Symptoms:	Lower Tolerance Level	66

67	Effects of Grief:	Grief Affects Everything	67
68	Effects of Grief:	Death is Part of Living	68
69	Signs & Symptoms:	Chaos Rules	69
70	Responsibilities:	Decisions	70
71	Recovery Tool:	Emotional Support	71
72	Signs & Symptoms:	Expected Death	72
73	Recovery Tool:	Religious Beliefs	73
74	Recovery Tool:	No One Understands	74
75	Recovery Tool:	Photographs	75
76	Recovery Tool:	A Child's Reaction	76
77	Complication:	Taboo Relationships	77
78	Recovery Tool:	Old Love Letters	78
79	Recovery Tool:	Reminiscing	79
80	Recovery Tool:	Recalling Memories	80
81	Recovery Tool:	Greeting Cards	81
82	Recovery Tool:	Thank You Cards	82
83	Recovery Tool:	Grief Recovery Success	83
84	Recovery Tool:	Grief Partners	84
85	Recovery Tool:	Overwhelmed	85
86	Recovery Myth:	Recovery Myths	86
87	Complication:	Delaying Grief	87
88	Complication:	Distracters & Maskers	88
89	Complication:	Losses	89
90	Guilt:	Change the Future	90
91	Adversity:	The Ultimate Adversity	91
92	Recovery Tool:	Journaling	92
93	Guilt:	Sibling Rivalry	93
94	Guilt:	Bully Siblings	94
95	Guilt:	Sibling Death	95
96	Guilt:	Surviving Bullies	96
97	Type of Loss	Pet Death	97
98	Type of Loss	Parental Parent	98
99	Complication:	Rejection	99
100	Complication:	Exclusion	100

GRIEF BRIEF 1

SIGNS & SYMPTOMS

FORGETTING MEMORIES

Visiting places or carrying objects that remind the survivor of the deceased is motivated through a fear of losing or forgetting precious memories.

Carrying tokens of affection has long been an accepted custom when one loves another.

One does not stop loving simply because their loved one has died.

If this custom is acceptable while living, why then would it not be acceptable once a loved one has died?

It may be that after a time, carrying tokens of remembrance or visiting special places may no longer be necessary for the survivor.

Until that time comes, and as long as the behavior does not become compulsive, visiting special places and carrying tokens of remembrance are perfectly normal and comforting.

NOTES

_____

_____

_____

_____

www.MourningCofee.com

(903) 796-9669

GRIEF BRIEF 2
SIGNS & SYMPTOMS
AILMENT OF THE SOUL

Grief is an ailment of the soul.

When the body suffers injury or ailment, one must take the time to recover or restore good physical health.

When one's soul suffers injury or ailment, one must take equal measures to restore health and psychological balance.

The question is often asked, "How long should it take to recover from the loss of a loved one?"

Length of recovery is based on several aspects.

The length, depth, and kinship of the relationship are all aspects that will affect the length of recovery.

One's psychological health, age, and past experiences with loss will also contribute to the speed at which one recovers.

NOTES

_____

_____

_____

_____

www.MourningCoffee.com

(903) 796-9669

GRIEF BRIEF 3
SIGNS & SYMPTOMS
GRIEF OR DEPRESSION

Grief and depression are different conditions.

With grief, the world looks poor and empty.

With depression, the person feels poor and empty.

Although depression may exist during bereavement, it seems to be a transient state.

If depression debilitates the bereaved for an extended period, professional practitioners might be considered.

If one has suffered an extended period of grief and notices that one's coping skills are not improving; or if one has thoughts of harming oneself, one might consider professional intervention.

NOTES
_____
_____
_____
_____
_____
_____
_____

www.MourningCoffee.com

(903) 796-9669

GRIEF BRIEF 4

SIGNS & SYMPTOMS

SLEEP DISTURBANCES

Sleep disturbances are common among survivors in the early stages of loss.

Early morning wake ups and difficulties falling asleep are generally experienced during the first four months after the loss of a significant loved one.

In normal grief, these symptoms seem to taper off, and medical intervention is not usually required.

NOTES

_____

_____

_____

_____

_____

_____

_____

_____

_____

www.MourningCoffee.com

(903) 796-9669

GRIEF BRIEF 5

SIGNS & SYMPTOMS

APPETITE DISTURBANCES

Appetite disturbances are very common during mourning.

They usually manifest themselves in terms of under eating rather than overeating.

Significant changes in eating habits may result in significant changes in weight.

Significant changes in weight in the elderly, in-firmed, and minors may be cause for concern.

If one feels that significant weight changes are cause for concern, consulting with one's physician may be advantageous.

NOTES

_____

_____

_____

_____

_____

_____

www.MourningCoffee.com

(903) 796-9669

GRIEF BRIEF 6
SIGNS & SYMPTOMS
ABSENTMINDEDNESS

Newly bereaved individuals may find that they are more absentminded than usual.

Absent-mindedness, in and of itself, is not cause for alarm.

If this behavior is extreme, individuals may find themselves causing great inconvenience or harm.

If this behavior manifests itself for an extended period, or is severe in consequence, one should consider consulting with a counselor.

NOTES

_____

_____

_____

_____

_____

_____

_____

_____

_____

www.MourningCoffee.com

(903) 796-9669

GRIEF BRIEF 7

COMPLICATION

SOCIAL WITHDRAWL

People who have recently lost a loved one may tend to withdraw from family or friends in intimate and social situations.

This tendency is generally brief and usually corrects itself without intervention.

If one continues to withdraw from social interactions over an extended length of time, one might find it comforting to consult with a counselor.

NOTES

_____

_____

_____

_____

_____

_____

_____

_____

_____

_____

www.MourningCoffee.com

(903) 796-9669

GRIEF BRIEF 8

SIGNS & SYMPTOMS

DREAMS OF THE DEAD

Dreams of the deceased are very common.

Sweet dreams and distressing dreams alike may indicate where one is within the cycle of grief recovery.

Commonly, dreams with unresolved issues indicate an inability toward resolution and may require professional intervention.

NOTES

_____

_____

_____

_____

_____

_____

_____

_____

_____

_____

www.MourningCoffee.com

(903) 796-9669

GRIEF BRIEF 9

COMPLICATION

PAINFUL TRIGGERS

Some survivors will avoid places or things that trigger painful feelings of grief.

Quick disposal of the decedent's belongings may indicate ambivalence and can result in complicated grief.

Survivors suffering extended avoidance or ambivalence might consider professional intervention.

NOTES

_____

_____

_____

_____

_____

_____

_____

_____

_____

www.MourningCoffee.com

(903) 796-9669

GRIEF BRIEF 10

SIGNS & SYMPTOMS

SEARCHING

Searching and calling out for the decedent is not unusual behavior.

Over time, it should subside.

NOTES

_____

_____

_____

_____

_____

_____

_____

_____

_____

_____

_____

_____

GRIEF BRIEF 11

SIGNS & SYMPTOMS

SIGHING

Sighing is a normal stress reducer and is normal among the recently bereaved.

It correlates closely with the feeling of breathlessness.

Over time, as one's bereavement subsides, so too should sighing.

NOTES

_____

_____

_____

_____

_____

_____

_____

_____

_____

_____

GRIEF BRIEF 12

SIGNS & SYMPTOMS

HYPERACTIVITY

Often time's recently bereaved survivors will have a period of restless hyperactivity.

One may find that projects that have gone years without completion are now easily accomplished.

One's house may be brightly and freshly clean, as may the garage.

Half-finished hobby projects and other back burner improvement projects may likewise suddenly be completed.

This is normal and should subside over time.

NOTES

_____

_____

_____

_____

_____

_____

_____

_____

www.MourningCoffee.com

(903) 796-9669

GRIEF BRIEF 13

SIGNS & SYMPTOMS

TEARS

It has been speculated that tears may have some healing potential.

The chemical imbalances caused by stress may be leveled out by the removal of toxic substances through tears.

Tears also put others on notice that the survivor is in need of understanding.

Over time, as stress diminishes, so too will flowing tears.

NOTES

_____

_____

_____

_____

_____

_____

_____

_____

www.MourningCoffee.com

(903) 796-9669

GRIEF BRIEF 14

COMPLICATION

MISTAKEN GRIEF

Grief is sometimes mistaken for depression.

While it is true that in both circumstances sleep disturbances, changes in appetite, and extreme sadness are experienced, the common loss of self-esteem found in depression is absent in grief.

If one suspects despair in a survivor, one should suggest counseling.

Do not take the responsibility of helping a survivor through depression upon yourself.

Depression needs to be treated by a professionally trained physician.

NOTES

_____

_____

_____

_____

_____

_____

_____

_____

GRIEF BRIEF 15

COMPLICATION

WORRY

Worry exacerbates fatigue and grief.

If you are experiencing the phases of grief, chances are, your unwelcome companion is worry.

Since worry exacerbates your experience, it can be a good practice to address your worries sooner rather than later.

If you find that your level of functionality interferes with your ability to settle logically your worries with sound and calming strategies, a trusted friend or experienced counselor might be able to assist you.

NOTES

_____

_____

_____

_____

_____

_____

_____

GRIEF BRIEF 16

EXPECTATION

MOURNING EQUALS ADAPTING

Grief is one's experiences after loss.

Mourning is the process of adapting to that loss.

NOTES

_____

_____

_____

_____

_____

_____

_____

_____

_____

_____

_____

_____

_____

www.MourningCoffee.com

(903) 796-9669

GRIEF BRIEF 17

EXPECTATION

PHASES OF MOURNING

PHASES OF MOURNING (Parkes)

1. Period of numbness

2. Yearning

3. Disorganization & despair

4. Reorganized behavior

NOTES

_____

_____

_____

_____

_____

_____

_____

_____

_____

_____

GRIEF BRIEF 18

EXPECTATION

TASKS OF MOURNING

TASKS OF MOURNING (Worden)

1.   Accepting the reality of loss

2.   Process the pain of loss

3.   Adjust to a world without the deceased

   a)   Internally

   b)   Externally

   c)   Spiritually

4.   Find an enduring connection with the deceased in your new life without them.

NOTES

_____

_____

_____

_____

_____

_____

_____

_____

www.MourningCoffee.com

(903) 796-9669

GRIEF BRIEF 19

EXPECTATION

GRIEF WORK

Grief is a cognitive process involving confrontation with and restructuring of thoughts about the deceased, the loss experience, and the changed world within which the bereaved must now live. (Stroebe, 1992)

Since mourning is a process, rather than a state of mind, the above statement implies that we must work to overcome the devastation of loss.

This activity is known as grief work.

NOTES

_____

_____

_____

_____

_____

_____

_____

_____

_____

GRIEF BRIEF 20

EXPECTATION

SADNESS

Sadness is the most common feeling experienced during bereavement. Persons, who block sadness with excessive activity, find that their sadness surfaces once they are exhausted.

Exhaustion renders one less able to overcome the intensity of sadness.

NOTES

_____

_____

_____

_____

_____

_____

_____

_____

_____

_____

www.MourningCoffee.com

(903) 796-9669

GRIEF BRIEF 21

SIGNS & SYMPTOMS

NUMBING OF SENSES

The numbing of our senses allows us to get through the immediate pain of our loss.

As time passes, the numbness will subside.

As this happens, you will realize that pain is its unwelcome replacement.

This evolution marks the onset of your grief experience.

NOTES

_____

_____

_____

_____

_____

_____

_____

_____

_____

_____

www.MourningCoffee.com

(903) 796-9669

GRIEF BRIEF 22

SIGNS & SYMPTOMS

HALLUCINATIONS

Both visual and auditory hallucinations are common during bereavement.

Although disconcerting to some, others find these experiences to be comforting.

The hallucinatory experience is generally transient, occurring within the first few weeks of loss.

Hallucinations are not an indication of a more complicated grief experience, nor do they allude to an extended grief experience.

NOTES

_____

_____

_____

_____

_____

_____

_____

_____

_____

www.MourningCoffee.com

(903) 796-9669

GRIEF BRIEF 23

SIGNS & SYMPTOMS

COMPETITIVE BEHAVIOR

Crying evokes sympathy from others and creates an atmosphere where competitive behaviors are suspended.

Competitive suspension allows the bereaved to function without undue worries and stresses outside of the bereavement recovery experience.

NOTES

_____

_____

_____

_____

_____

_____

_____

_____

_____

_____

_____

www.MourningCoffee.com

(903) 796-9669

GRIEF BRIEF 24

STAGE OF GRIEF

ANGER

Anger is common among the bereaved.

It is generally brought on through anxiety, panic, and frustration.

It is important to properly direct anger at the grim reaper rather than toward others.

Realizing that the absence of your loved one has caused your emotional issues will help you move beyond the anger and develop the necessary skills for recovery.

The most dangerous adaptation to intense anger is to turn on oneself.

Mourners who inflict their anger on themselves run the risk of developing self-loathing and in more severe cases, may fall prey to suicide.

If you are suffering extreme anger for an extended time and find that you are unable to control yourself emotionally or physically, consider seeking immediate assistance.

NOTES

_____

_____

www.MourningCoffee.com

(903) 796-9669

GRIEF BRIEF 25

COMPLICATION

GUILT

Guilt is common among survivors.

Usually, guilt is equated to something that did or did not transpire in connection to the death.

Guilt is generally irrational and dissipates itself through reality adjustments.

If guilt is justifiably connected to the death, intervention counseling should be engaged as soon as possible.

NOTES

_____

_____

_____

_____

_____

_____

_____

_____

_____

25

GRIEF BRIEF 26

SIGNS & SYMPTOMS

ANXIETY

Anxiety is common among the bereaved.

A survivor may fear that without the support of the deceased, they will perish.

This may create a heightened sense of personal death awareness.

As ones skills adjust to the absence of their loved one, so too should anxiety.

In the interim survivors may find comfort in consulting a grief expert.

NOTES

_____

_____

_____

_____

_____

_____

_____

_____

_____

www.MourningCoffee.com

(903) 796-9669

GRIEF BRIEF 27

SIGNS & SYMPTOMS

LONELINESS

Loneliness is frequently expressed by the bereaved, especially by those who have lost their spouses.

Social loneliness may be curbed through social support.

Emotional loneliness, however, is brought on by a broken attachment.

With such, a new attachment is the only remedy.

Certain survivors are unwilling to form new attachments and thereby endure sever loneliness indefinitely.

This behavior is more common among the elderly.

NOTES

_____

_____

_____

_____

_____

_____

_____

www.MourningCoffee.com

(903) 796-9669

GRIEF BRIEF 28

SIGNS & SYMPTOMS

FATIGUE

Survivors frequently experience fatigue.

To some, fatigue is unexpected and thereby distressing.

An ordinarily active person may find that they are very confused by such an experience.

When fatigue becomes debilitating, one should consider professional intervention.

NOTES

_____

_____

_____

_____

_____

_____

_____

_____

_____

GRIEF BRIEF 29

SIGNS & SYMPTOMS

HELPLESSNESS

Widows, in particular, experience feelings of help-lessness.

It is not uncommon for widows to suffer such feelings for an extended period of time.

Family and friends play an important rehabilitative role during this period of insecurity.

This role may be minimal as in morale encouragement.

It may, however, be extensive and require a more hands-on approach, leading up to and including daily functional participation.

NOTES

_____

_____

_____

_____

_____

_____

GRIEF BRIEF 30

COMPLICATION

FEELINGS OF EMANCIPATION

In a situation of abuse or neglect, feelings of emancipation are often a welcome relief.

If you witness an emancipatory type behavior in the recently bereaved, realize that it is likely the result of liberty from horrific experiences.

This person may need great understanding and gentle reconstruction of their self-esteem, self-value, and self-worth.

Juvenile behaviors may be underlying, and professional guidance and/or intervention might be helpful.

NOTES

_____

_____

_____

_____

_____

_____

_____

_____

www.MourningCoffee.com

(903) 796-9669

GRIEF BRIEF 31

SIGNS & SYMPTOMS

SHOCK

Shock is generally experienced whenever a death occurs.

Even if your loved one suffered a life-ending illness, the exact moment of death remains unpredictable.

Therefore, the notice that death has occurred may for a brief moment, be shocking.

Shock occurs most often and is lingering, in the case of sudden or unexpected death.

NOTES

GRIEF BRIEF 32

SIGNS & SYMPTOMS

YEARNING

Yearning for the deceased is natural, especially among widows.

When yearning diminishes, one may conclude that mourning is coming to an end.

A common term for this is "closure."

Although one may accomplish closure, it is important to realize that anniversaries and holidays may continue to be difficult days to experience.

NOTES

_____

_____

_____

_____

_____

_____

_____

_____

_____

www.MourningCoffee.com

(903) 796-9669

GRIEF BRIEF 33

GUILT

RELIEF

Family and close friends may feel great relief at the passing of a loved one who suffered a lengthy illness or painful death.

Quite often, feelings of guilt accompany their relief.

It may be helpful to realize that feelings of relief at the ending of great suffering are born from empathy and compassion.

Both empathy and compassion are selfless human emotions.

NOTES

_____

_____

_____

_____

_____

_____

_____

_____

_____

GRIEF BRIEF 34

RECOVERY TOOLS

SHARE YOUR STORY

Mourners want and need most of all, to talk about their loss.

They need to work through what has happened to them.

Talking with someone who knows them and will not judge them allows them to:

a) accept that death has happened,

b) realize that there is a new reality in which they must function, and

c) redirects them to work out their road to recovery.

NOTES

_____

_____

_____

_____

_____

_____

_____

GRIEF BRIEF 35

COMPLICATION

FROZEN IMPERFECTION

While it is true that none of us is perfect, at the moment of death, imperfection is frozen.

Unfinished business remains unfinished.

Estrangement remains estranged.

Meanness remains mean, etc.

Death robs the living of the opportunity for resolution and blocks the comfort of peace.

NOTES

_____

_____

_____

_____

_____

_____

_____

_____

www.MourningCoffee.com

(903) 796-9669

GRIEF BRIEF 36
RECOVERY TOOL
EXERCISE

Exercise is good for the heart, body and soul.

A 20 to 40-minute aerobic activity results in improvement in the survivor's state of mind.

A vigorous pumping heart decreases anxiety, lifts the mood and creates a positive experience that persists for several hours.

Psychological benefits associated with exercise are a welcome bonus for the bereaved.

They are comparable to the gains found with standard forms of psychotherapy.

NOTES

_____

_____

_____

_____

_____

_____

_____

_____

GRIEF BRIEF 37

RECOVERY TOOL

RELIGION

Religion offers hope for the future and forgiveness for the past.

It also offers like-minded support and understanding.

It can be a source for counseling and re-socialization, a gateway for grief recovery.

NOTES

_____

_____

_____

_____

_____

_____

_____

_____

_____

_____

_____

www.MourningCoffee.com

(903) 796-9669

GRIEF BRIEF 38

RECOVERY TOOL

FRIENDS AND FAMILY

Family and friends can be a great resource for grief recovery.

Traveling to visit loved ones in other areas or having them visit the survivor, offers companionship that is familiar, uplifting, and relative to their life's experiences.

NOTES

_____

_____

_____

_____

_____

_____

_____

_____

_____

_____

GRIEF BRIEF 39

RECOVERY TOOL

HOBBIES

Hobbies occupy the mind and hands.

They engage our brains and keep them in good health.

Hobbies create a sense of accomplishment.

They propel us toward a healthier and happier grief recovery.

NOTES

_____

_____

_____

_____

_____

_____

_____

_____

_____

GRIEF BRIEF 40

SUPPORT

PSYCHOTHERAPY

For complicated grief, psychotherapy is sometimes warranted.

Counseling can help a survivor identify unhealthy habits and encourage positive growth.

It can yield a recovery plan that the survivor is unable to identify, implement, and accomplish on his or her own.

NOTES

_____

_____

_____

_____

_____

_____

_____

_____

_____

_____

www.MourningCoffee.com

(903) 796-9669

GRIEF BRIEF 41

SUPPORT

SUPPORT GROUP

A support group is a scheduled gathering of people with common experiences and concerns.

It provides emotional and moral support, as well as new perspectives on life, increased understanding of grief, and close personal ties.

NOTES

_____

_____

_____

_____

_____

_____

_____

_____

_____

_____

www.MourningCoffee.com

(903) 796-9669

GRIEF BRIEF 42

RECOVERY TOOL

TRADITIONS

Traditions are a wonderful tool for grief recovery.

Observing traditions that were once enjoyed with the deceased helps us accept that they are gone from us physically, yet with us still, through the activities and love we shared together.

Such activities, now traditions, will aid your family by anchoring them securely to their heritage.

Observing traditions stabilizes a family through loss, expansion, and changing environments.

NOTES

_____

_____

_____

_____

_____

_____

_____

_____

www.MourningCoffee.com

(903) 796-9669

GRIEF BRIEF 43

RECOVERY TOOL
ANIMAL COMPANIONSHIP

Animal companionship typically results in fewer migraines and less persistent fears.

Fewer phobias, lower levels of panic, and less drug and alcohol intake are very positive side effects associated with our furry friends.

The love and acceptance of a pet help us combat depression and isolation.

If you have a family pet, be mindful of their needs.

Taking Fido out for a brisk walk will provide both of you healthier opportunities for exercise, socialization, and companionship.

NOTES

_____

_____

_____

_____

_____

_____

www.MourningCoffee.com

(903) 796-9669

GRIEF BRIEF 44

COMPLICATION

BREAKDOWN

Eventually, people who avoid all aspects of conscious grief will break down.

Due to their denial, some form of depression usually brings on the breakdown.

At this juncture, it may be advantageous to seek professional guidance for recovery assistance.

NOTES

_____

_____

_____

_____

_____

_____

_____

_____

_____

_____

GRIEF BRIEF 45

COMPLICATION

DELAYED GRIEF

Delayed grief is usually more difficult to overcome.

Not only is depression more prevalent, the survivor is faced with a less supportive social system than would have been available at the time of loss.

Delayed grief sometimes calls for professional assistance and guidance. NOTES

_____

_____

_____

_____

_____

_____

_____

_____

_____

_____

_____

GRIEF BRIEF 46

RECOVERY TOOL

DEVELOPING NEW SKILLS

Many survivors resent having to develop new skills that were once performed by their deceased loved one.

This is a normal reaction to your loss.

The key to recovery is to either learn the skill yourself or find someone who will do it for you.

In both scenarios, your reward is growth, either personally or socially.

In both circumstances, your movement toward recovery is positive

NOTES

_____

_____

_____

_____

_____

_____

_____

_____

GRIEF BRIEF 47

COMPLICATION

REBUILDING ONESELF

Recovering from grief often entails the rebuilding of oneself.

If one has been in a marriage for fifty years or so, their identity has generally morphed into that of a couple.

Being alone after such a long period of time, may take quite an adjustment.

NOTES

_____

_____

_____

_____

_____

_____

_____

_____

_____

GRIEF BRIEF 48

COMPLICATION

FUNCTIONALITY

On average, a widow tends to begin the realization that she must function on her own 3 – 4 months following the death of her husband.

Men, on the other hand, do not adjust as easily as do women.

Therefore, a widower takes longer to realize and begin adjustments in functionality than do widows.

NOTES

_____

_____

_____

_____

_____

_____

_____

_____

_____

www.MourningCoffee.com

(903) 796-9669

GRIEF BRIEF 49

STAGE OF RECOVERY

ACCEPT REALITY

The first task of grieving is to accept the reality that your loved one is dead, that they are gone, and that they will not return.

NOTES

_____

_____

_____

_____

_____

_____

_____

_____

_____

_____

_____

_____

www.MourningCoffee.com

(903) 796-9669

GRIEF BRIEF 50

STAGEOF RECOVERY

ACCEPT DEATH

The funeral is an important factor in accepting the death of an individual.

Without the acceptance that death has occurred, the survivor enters into a state of loneliness.

A prolonged state of loneliness ushers in isolation.

Extended isolation will metamorphose into depression.

Once depression occurs, grief recovery becomes increasingly more difficult to overcome.

It is at this juncture, one might act upon opportunities for professional assistance.

NOTES

_____

_____

_____

_____

_____

_____

_____

www.MourningCoffee.com

(903) 796-9669

GRIEF BRIEF 51

RECOVERY TOOL

MEN AND WOMEN EXPRESS THEMSELVES DIFFERENTLY

Men and women express themselves differently.

This fact is magnified in a grief situation.

Men may not feel free to openly express the depth of their grief.

Societal mores allow women much more latitude in their expression of grief.

NOTES

_____

_____

_____

_____

_____

_____

_____

_____

_____

GRIEF BRIEF 52

RECOVERY TOOL

GRIEF EXPRESSION AND RECOVERY

Religion is often the determining factor when it comes to grief expression and recovery.

NOTES

---

(903) 796-9669

GRIEF BRIEF 53

RECOVERY TOOL

PATIENCE

Recovery from the death of a loved one may take a long time, especially in immediate family situations.

It is imperative to understand that patience plays a large role in grief work.

Be patient with yourself, with others trying to help, and with those not realizing that you need help.

NOTES

_____

_____

_____

_____

_____

_____

_____

_____

_____

GRIEF BRIEF 54

COMPLICATION

EMOTIONAL ROLLER COASTER

Grief is the ultimate emotional roller coaster ride.

Do not be discouraged if you have a few great days and then experience several bad ones.

Do not think of this as a setback.

Alternating good and bad days is a normal grief experience.

You will find that as time goes by, you will eventually experience more good days than bad.

NOTES

_____

_____

_____

_____

_____

_____

_____

_____

www.MourningCoffee.com

(903) 796-9669

GRIEF BRIEF 55

COMPLICATION

PSYCHOLOGICAL DISTRESS

Grief creates psychological distress and turmoil.

Awareness of one's own discrepancies does not make the grief experience easier; it does, however, offer self-analysis, and thereby the development of additional coping techniques and skills.

Psychological distress can be dangerous and rather perplexing.

If you or someone you know finds psychological distress is or is becoming a reality, consider professional assistance sooner rather than later.

An ounce of prevention is worth a pound of cure when approaching this dangerous cliff.

NOTES

_____

_____

_____

_____

_____

_____

_____

GRIEF BRIEF 56

COMPLICATION

STRESSFUL IMPACT

Grief is stressful.

Stress has a negative impact on one's immune system.

When suffering the loss of a loved one, it is a good idea to notify your primary care physician if you have existing physical, psychological or emotional conditions.

NOTES

_____

_____

_____

_____

_____

_____

_____

_____

_____

GRIEF BRIEF 57

COMPLICATION

FREQUENT AILMENTS

Many bereaved individuals experience more frequent occurrences of ailments.

Common complaints are additional colds, lingering flu, headaches, stomach upset, back and neck pain, indigestion, insomnia, and flare-ups of pre-existing conditions.

This is normal during the phases of grief.

It is recommended that survivors notify their physician if these ailments become intolerable.

NOTES

_____

_____

_____

_____

_____

_____

_____

_____

_____

www.MourningCoffee.com

(903) 796-9669

GRIEF BRIEF 58

COMPLICATION

SPECIAL DAYS

Holidays, birthdays, anniversaries and especially the yearly loss anniversary, are extremely stressful for survivors of loss.

The anticipation of these important dates may sometimes be worse than the day itself.

If you have a close friend or relative, it may be a good idea to let them know that you might need extra understanding and support on these days.

NOTES

_____

_____

_____

_____

_____

_____

_____

_____

_____

GRIEF BRIEF 59

COMPLICATION

DECREASED FUNCTIONALITY

A grief-stricken person is unable to function at their usual 100% capability. It is therefore wise to postpone major decisions at this time.

Selling a home, moving to another city, or changing jobs or professions, are all better put off to some later date if possible.

NOTES

_____

_____

_____

_____

_____

_____

_____

_____

_____

_____

_____

www.MourningCoffee.com

(903) 796-9669

GRIEF BRIEF 60

PRE-OCCUPATION

FORGETFULNESS

During bereavement, one may find that they are more forgetful than usual.

This is caused by the preoccupation of grief.

Lost car keys, misplaced purses, forgotten appointments, etc., are normal occurrences during this time.

It is a good practice to begin writing things down on a list.

It is important to realize your memory is suffering the ill effects of stress brought on by grief. You may find that you cannot remember if you have completed your tasks list successfully.

It is therefore recommended that you check tasks off as they are accomplished.

NOTES

_____

_____

_____

_____

_____

GRIEF BRIEF 61

PRE-OCCUPATION

DISORGANIZATION OF THOUGHTS

Due to a disorganization of thoughts during bereavement, tasks may take longer, or be more difficult to complete.

Sometimes, writing down the steps necessary before beginning a task, helps one complete it more satisfactorily.

NOTES

_____

_____

_____

_____

_____

_____

_____

_____

_____

_____

www.MourningCoffee.com

(903) 796-9669

GRIEF BRIEF 62

PRE-OCCUPATION

DIFFICULTIES CONCENTRATING

During bereavement, concentrating and retaining information becomes difficult.

This is caused by a preoccupation of loss.

Reading and other tasks requiring concentration may take longer than usual.

Mistakes and errors may also become more prevalent.

As time passes, mistakes lessen and the ability to concentrate and retain information returns.

NOTES

_____

_____

_____

_____

_____

_____

_____

_____

_____

GRIEF BRIEF 63

PRE-OCCUPATION

LOWER FUNCTIONALITY

During the early stages of bereavement, preoccupation of your loss interferes with your ability to function at your normal capacity.

One's mind wanders, and it becomes difficult to stay focused or on task.

As life reorganizes itself, so too will one's level of functionality.

NOTES

_____

_____

_____

_____

_____

_____

_____

_____

_____

www.MourningCoffee.com

(903) 796-9669

GRIEF BRIEF 64

PRE-OCCUPATION

DO NOT DRIVE

Driving is especially dangerous during the early stages of bereavement.

One's mind will wander, and suddenly one is where he or she was going without noticing the drive there.

It is common for recently bereaved individuals to run traffic lights and stop signs.

Traffic reports indicate an increase in missing turns and traffic accidents during this time as well.

Be extra careful if you must drive, but it is recommended that you engage someone else to run your errands for a while.

NOTES

_____

_____

_____

_____

_____

_____

www.MourningCoffee.com

(903) 796-9669

GRIEF BRIEF 65

PRE-OCCUPATION

LACK OF INTEREST

During grief, the survivor may feel a lack of interest or motivation.

What was once of great importance may seem meaningless for quite some time.

As the survivor passes through the different phases of mourning, the preoccupation of loss causing the lack of interest and motivation will become less prevalent.

Eventually, the survivor will return to his or her pre-loss level of interest and motivation.

NOTES

_____

_____

_____

_____

_____

_____

_____

_____

www.MourningCoffee.com

(903) 796-9669

GRIEF BRIEF 66

SIGNS & SYMPTOMS

LOWER TOLERANCE LEVEL

During bereavement, it is common to experience a lower tolerance level.

One's patience may not be what it used to be.

Minor irritations may have the ability to overwhelm the survivor.

As the survivor accepts, adjusts, and becomes accustomed to their new life without the deceased, irritability should subside.

NOTES

_____

_____

_____

_____

_____

_____

_____

_____

_____

www.MourningCoffee.com

(903) 796-9669

GRIEF BRIEF 67

EFFECTS OF LOSS

GRIEF AFFECTS ALL ASPECTS

Grief is overwhelming and affects all aspects of the survivor's life.

Lack of sleep, loss of appetite, and a feeling of despair are normal reactions to loss.

These experiences can contribute to extreme fatigue which may lead to chronic fatigue.

If you find that you are unable to motivate yourself for an extended period, you might consider consulting with your physician.

NOTES

_____

_____

_____

_____

_____

_____

_____

_____

_____

GRIEF BRIEF 68

EFFECTS OF LOSS

DEATH IS PART OF LIVING

Although death is a part of living, life does not prepare us for this experience.

Unfortunately, we only realize this when we experience the death of a loved one.

In due time, you will learn how to survive this devastation and your life will one day be better.

NOTES

_____

_____

_____

_____

_____

_____

_____

_____

_____

_____

www.MourningCoffee.com

(903) 796-9669

GRIEF BRIEF 69

SIGNS & SYMPTOMS

CHAOS RULES

When a loved one dies, if pre-arrangements have not been settled chaos rules your mind.

There are an infinite number of decisions to make at this time.

It may seem as though your world has been turned upside down.

You may be frightened, angry, hurt, alone, confused, and facing life altering decisions at this juncture.

Making sound decisions that will affect the rest of your life, and the lives of other survivors, is a profound responsibility.

Unfortunately, if pre-arrangements were not settled, you will be faced with this task at a most confusing and difficult time.

NOTES

_____

_____

_____

_____

_____

www.MourningCoffee.com

(903) 796-9669

GRIEF BRIEF 70

RESPONSIBILITES

DECISIONS

At the time of death, the next of kin must make decisions that will usher in and set the groundwork for the grief recovery experience for friends and family of the deceased.

They must be mindful that their choices will affect the memories and recollections that will either hamper or encourage healing for those left behind.

All of this must be accomplished under extreme pressure while adjusting to the fact that their loved one has died.

NOTES

_____

_____

_____

_____

_____

_____

_____

_____

GRIEF BRIEF 71

SUPPORT

EMOTIONAL SUPPORT

Following the death of a loved one, there may be a significant need to reach out for emotional support.

This can be accomplished through a support group, an understanding cleric, a professional funeral practitioner, or a therapist.

How do you know if you need professional assistance?

If you find that you have unanswered questions or that you need a tool to help you cope with the loss, you might benefit from professional support.

When you break your limb you go to a qualified care professional for proper wound care.

Why wouldn't you go to a qualified care professional when your life has broken?

Qualified wound care is just as important for your soul as it is for your limb.

NOTES

_____

_____

_____

GRIEF BRIEF 72

SIGNS & SYMPTOMS

EXPECTED DEATH

Grief accompanies expected death.

As with a long-term illness, you will still experience emotional and physical grief with expected death.

NOTES

_____

_____

_____

_____

_____

_____

_____

_____

_____

_____

_____

www.MourningCoffee.com

(903) 796-9669

GRIEF BRIEF 73

RECOVERY TOOL

RELIGIOUS BELIEFS

Religious beliefs are often called into question at a time of loss.

Some find it helpful to speak with a faithful friend or their clergy for added strength during this time.

Still, others find it best to rely on quiet faith.

You are the only person who can determine the best course of action in this situation.

NOTES

_____

_____

_____

_____

_____

_____

_____

_____

_____

_____

GRIEF BRIEF 74

RECOVERY TOOL

NO ONE UNDERSTANDS

Teenagers often feel that parents and teachers do not understand them.

Who then does one turn to for help as a teenager?

The best person for the job is someone who actively listens, asks questions, and does not criticize.

NOTES

_____

_____

_____

_____

_____

_____

_____

_____

_____

_____

www.MourningCoffee.com

(903) 796-9669

GRIEF BRIEF 75
RECOVERY TOOL
PHOTOGRAPHS

Photographs of activities shared with the deceased are wonderful tools for grief recovery.

They help us realize that we have many wonderful memories to draw upon giving us comfort that our loved one will never be forgotten.

NOTES

_____

_____

_____

_____

_____

_____

_____

_____

_____

GRIEF BRIEF 76

RECOVERY TOOL

A CHILD'S REACTION

A child's reaction to death is predicated upon his or her experiences in life.

Losing favorite toys, moving away from friends, or the death of pets, serve to strengthen a child's inner fortitude while they are growing into their teenage years and adulthood.

Although these experiences can be upsetting, with a strong and loving family structure, a child may overcome these setbacks and emerge a stronger person.

These same disappointments and setbacks suffered in childhood, prepare children to face even greater tragedies such as betrayal, deception, and the death of loved ones as they mature.

NOTES

_____

_____

_____

_____

_____

_____

GRIEF BRIEF 77

COMPLICATION

TABOO RELATIONSHIPS

Taboo relationships present difficult grief recovery situations for surviving lovers and surviving family members.

If the taboo relationship was unaccepted or unknown by the decedent's family, the surviving lover may find resentment or exclusion greets them as they approach the surviving family.

They may find that they are not welcome at services or mentioned in the obituary.

Taboo relationships may include infidelity, same sex attraction, pedophilia attraction, under class attraction, and associations with lawless individuals.

If you find yourself in this type of situation, you might look for support from others who knew and accepted your relationship with the decedent.

If this is not possible, a therapist who specializes in these types of grief relationships may be your best option.

NOTES

_____

_____

GRIEF BRIEF 78

RECOVERY TOOL

OLD LOVE LETTERS

Old love letters received from our loved one offers us private time for reflection.

At the appropriate time, they are wonderful tools that promote grief recovery.

They help us understand that the experiences we shared together are not gone; they live within our hearts and minds.

They help us move the deceased from a living participant in our lives into a loving memory.

One must judge for oneself when the appropriate time arrives.

NOTES

_____

_____

_____

_____

_____

_____

_____

www.MourningCoffee.com

(903) 796-9669

GRIEF BRIEF 79

RECOVERY TOOL

REMINISCING

Reminiscing with others who loved the deceased helps us to recall treasured moments and validates their value.

Loving stories of fond memories bring comfort and joy to our hearts.

Sharing and recalling these treasured moments that were once enjoyed with the deceased, help us accept that they are gone from us physically yet with us still, through the activities and love they shared with others.

NOTES

_____

_____

_____

_____

_____

_____

_____

_____

www.MourningCoffee.com

(903) 796-9669

GRIEF BRIEF 80

RECOVERY TOOL

RECALLING MEMORIES

Recalling fond memories will aid your grief recovery by anchoring your decedent securely to your heritage.

Observing traditions stabilizes a family through loss, expansion, and changing environments.

NOTES

_____

_____

_____

_____

_____

_____

_____

_____

_____

_____

_____

GRIEF BRIEF 81

RECOVERY TOOL

GREETING CARDS

Greeting cards received from our loved ones are treasures that should be revisited.

Reading your loved one's words written to you from the past helps you to understand that their love was and remains very special in your heart.

Greeting cards also help you to realize that your loved one's message to you remains alive.

Reading these cards offers comfort that you will not forget your loved one and helps you realize that you can now live on without them by your side.

There may eventually come a day when you will no longer find it necessary to read these cards as frequently as you once did.

NOTES

_____

_____

_____

_____

_____

GRIEF BRIEF 82

RECOVERY TOOL

THANK YOU CARDS

Thank you cards written to your loved one from others are wonderful to read for grief recovery.

They help you know that others recognized and appreciated your loved one's fine qualities.

They also help you remember the kindnesses your loved one offered to others.

They offer tangible proof that your loved one existed, that he/she was a good person, and that he/she was appreciated.

They also give you comfort that you will not forget your loved one, nor his/her accomplishments.

NOTES

_____

_____

_____

_____

_____

_____

_____

www.MourningCoffee.com

(903) 796-9669

GRIEF BRIEF 83

RECOVERY TOOL

GRIEF RECOVERY SUCCESS

Success in moving through grief depends on your willingness to recover.

If you are the type of person that enjoys or thrives on being a victim, you will most likely travel very slowly through recovery.

You must decide that you want to recover, that you are willing to move your loved one into a memory, and that you are going to overcome your heartache.

Without these decisions, you will remain trapped within your own recurring grief cycle indefinitely.

NOTES

_____

_____

_____

_____

_____

_____

_____

GRIEF BRIEF 84

RECOVERY TOOL

GRIEF PARTNERS

Pairing off with a grief partner can sometimes be helpful.

If you have a friend, an acquaintance, or a family member that has experienced and recovered from grief, they may be very helpful in guiding you through the path of grief recovery.

NOTES

_____

_____

_____

_____

_____

_____

_____

_____

_____

_____

GRIEF BRIEF 85
RECOVERY TOOL
OVERWHELMED

The death of a loved one can be overwhelming.

It is okay to feel overwhelmed when overwhelming events occur in your life.

If you have someone you can trust, it is sometimes helpful to allow him or her to handle some of your day-to-day responsibilities.

Simple things like doing the laundry may, for a time, be too much to accomplish.

Allow this trusted person to help you by doing these simple tasks that do not require your particular attention.

Doing so, also helps others to heal through service.

NOTES

_____

_____

_____

_____

_____

_____

_____

GRIEF BRIEF 86

RECOVERY MYTH

RECOVERY MYTHS

It is neither necessary, nor realistic to rely on mythical information about grief recovery.

One should realize that there will be days when they will fall apart, cry, or be cranky.

Keeping a stiff upper lip, getting a hold of yourself, not falling apart, and pulling yourself up by your bootstraps are mythical wishes when dealing with grief.

You will find that you will suffer these moments of weakness.

They are natural and allow the healing process to begin.

As time passes and you move your loved one into a loving memory, accepting that they are gone, and adjusting to your new life without them, you will find that these episodes will manifest themselves less often.

NOTES

_____

_____

_____

_____

_____

GRIEF BRIEF 87

COMPLICATION

DELAYING GRIEF

Delaying your grief does not eradicate it.

Delaying your grief only serves to extend and exacerbate your experience.

Delayed grief becomes complicated grief.

Once a survivor enters into a state of complicated grief, other issues come into play.

Often a survivor suffering complicated grief develops physical aliments.

These ailments, if left unattended, can turn into disease.

The same holds true for psychological ailments.

Even with treatment, if the underlying issue of grief is not addressed, these issues will become recurring.

NOTES

_____

_____

_____

_____

_____

GRIEF BRIEF 88

COMPLICATION

DISTRACTERS & MASKERS

Some mourners try to minimize or avoid their grief with distracters and/or maskers.

Popular distracters include food, excessive exercise, anger, isolation, sex, shopping, work, movies, books, and TV.

Popular maskers include alcohol, prescription drugs, over the counter drugs, and illegal drugs.

Self-medicating is never appropriate as it has a tendency to take control of your life and in no way contributes to recovery. It may also be very dangerous to your health and well being.

If you find that you are spending excessive hours in the afore mentioned distracters you might reevaluate your coping skills.

At some point, you need to realize that you are delaying your grief experience and that it may soon turn into complicated grief.

NOTES

_____

_____

_____

www.MourningCoffee.com

(903) 796-9669

GRIEF BRIEF 89

COMPLICATION

LOSSES

Death is the loss of life.

In the loss of a loved one, it is followed by grief.

Death is not the only issue a survivor suffers at the time of loss.

The loss of companionship, love, security, hopes, dreams, expectations, and many others are suffered by the survivor and attack their well-being.

It is important to recognize that you are suffering a vast array of issues at the loss of a significant loved one.

Recognition of these issues helps you to face them directly so that you may overcome them.

Recovery may require active redirecting of your future goals.

Some may find that their social status must also adjust.

Although there are many who love you and wish they could ease your pain, no one can accomplish your recovery except for you.

NOTES

GRIEF BRIEF 90

GUILT

CHANGE THE FUTURE

At the loss of a loved one, it is easy to feel guilty.

Perhaps you did not tell your loved one how much they meant to you. Perhaps you were not cooperative in making them as happy as they could have been. Perhaps you filled your days with activities away from home and their companionship. There are an infinite number of issues that create guilt for survivors.

Guilt brought on at a loved one's death is often regret. It is impossible to go back and change what you did or did not do, with or without your deceased loved one. It is possible, however, to change the future.

You might change the time spend with your loved ones remaining in your life. You might change the way you communicate your feelings. You might also influence other loved ones to express their love and compassion more openly so that when they are faced with loss, they do not suffer such intense regret.

Changing your future and the future of others so that they do not suffer intense regret at the time of loss is a great gift to them. They may not, however, realize what you have done for them until you are gone as well.

NOTES

_____

_____

GRIEF BRIEF 91

ADVERSITY

THE ULTIMATE ADVERSITY

Love is tempered and grows stronger through adversity and sacrifice.

The more we experience together the stronger our relationships become.

Death eradicates our ability to be together and to continue experiencing life together.

It does not, however, eradicate our ability to continue loving our decedent.

It does not make it impossible for our love to continue on and deepen as we continue through life without our companion or our loved one.

Love is not a physical experience - it is a deeply emotional and spiritual experience.

Were it not so, how would one explain the love a parent has for an unborn child?

How would one explain the abiding love parents carry to their graves for their miscarried children?

Death is the ultimate adversary in our relationships.

It does not, however, sever us from the love we hold dear in our hearts.

NOTES

_____

_____

GRIEF BRIEF 92

RECOVERY TOOL

JOURNALING

Journaling is an amazingly successful tool, whose application catapults a survivor from debilitating grief toward recovery.

It allows the survivor to record their fondest memories of their loved one.

It offers comfort and testimony that their memories were true experiences.

It helps to organize the mind when disorganization rules one's current world.

It ensures that as time clouds the mind written references are available for review.

It helps to relieve the stresses of debilitating loneliness, track one's progress in their healing journey, and offers tangible proof that improvement has been accomplished.

Journaling is a gift we give ourselves.

NOTES

_____

_____

_____

_____

www.MourningCoffee.com

(903) 796-9669

GRIEF BRIEF 93

GUILT

SIBLING RIVALRY

There are special issues that come into play at the death of a sibling.

If rivalry existed during the life of your sibling, expect to feel relief or extreme guilt at their passing.

These feelings are normal and will equalize as you recover from your loss.

NOTES

_____

_____

_____

_____

_____

_____

_____

_____

_____

_____

GRIEF BRIEF 94

GUILT

BULLY SIBLINGS

If your sibling was a bully, you might feel great relief upon their death.

The relief one experiences at this time is the realization that they no longer must continue experiencing domination and abuse.

You may also feel guilt over such relief.

Feelings of emancipation over the liberation from abuse are normal.

The guilt associated over these feelings should be temporary and equalize as time passes.

NOTES

_____

_____

_____

_____

_____

_____

_____

_____

www.MourningCoffee.com

(903) 796-9669

GRIEF BRIEF 95

GUILT

SIBLING DEATH

If your sibling was outgoing and popular and you existed in their shadow, you may feel, at long last, that you are no longer invisible in your social group or family structure. You may feel relief and guilt over these feelings and emotions.

These feelings are normal and are not cause for alarm. They are most likely fleeting thoughts that should instantly correct themselves.

One should not feel guilty over their momentary relief at the death of a competitive sibling. The momentary relief is generally replaced with sorrow at their loss.

As long as this normal course of recovery is accomplished, counseling is not necessary.

If prolonged guilt or extended oppression lingers, one's self-esteem may improve from consulting with a counselor. In such a case, self-esteem wounds are likely to affect the grief recovery experience.

To avert a complicated grief recovery experience, it is best not to delay counseling.

With children, recovery may be more difficult as their guilt scenarios may have unrealistic concepts.

In this case, counseling is most likely essential.

NOTES

GRIEF BRIEF 96

GUILT

SURVIVING BULLIES

If you are guilty of bullying a loved one who is now deceased, you may realize the full brunt of your abuse at their passing. Extreme feelings of guilt may plague your emotional and psychological health.

One must realize that the past cannot be changed. The future, however, is wide open for change.

If you are having feelings of guilt for bullying a loved one, take actions to change your behavior toward others immediately. Attribute your positive behavioral adjustments toward your loved one's memory. In so doing, you will better be able to recover from your past behavior and move forward in a positive healing direction.

Some bullies are unable to accept responsibility for their oppressive behavior. They may be narcissistic and incapable or non-desirous of realizing that their behaviors are inhumane. Bullies are overly "shame-prone". If a bully does not seek counseling at the passing of the person they have bullied, shame will eventually creep in and psychologically destroy them. This may result in a broken individual with reclusive tendencies or send them over the top, increasing their voracious bullying until they find themselves alone in the world. Neither scenario is a positive result. Whether you realize your guilt or not, counseling for a bully is essential.

NOTES

GRIEF BRIEF 97

TYPE OF LOSS

PET DEATH

As with family and friends, the death of a pet may be equally painful. The grief experience with human loss is predicated upon the depth of association. The same holds true for our animal companions.

Animal companions may have taken the place of past loved ones. They may even be the central emotional contact within our lives. They may be our best friends, our confidants, or our only contact with another living soul for weeks on end.

If your animal companion is an integral part of your existence, expect to grieve their loss as you would any other dear friend or loved one. You will most likely experience every phase of the grief cycle during recovery.

You may opt to bury your pet without ceremony. You may choose to bury your pet with memorial or funeral services. You may even choose to cremate your pet and have their cremains buried with you at your time of passing.

Whatever your final choices are for your pet's interment, realize that the passing of your animal companion may be just as debilitating as the loss of you human companions.

NOTES

_____

_____

GRIEF BRIEF 98

TYPE OF LOSS

LOSS OF A PARENT

The loss of a parent at any age is debilitating to their child's core strength.

The loss of parental security is devastating at two years old or at 32 years old.

A parental loss may result in the loss of your greatest champion, your provider, your friend, your confident, your favorite person ever, your emotional strength, and your protector. These losses are overwhelming for children and adults alike.

The loss of a parent may present an opportunity for self-evaluation, self-improvement, and inner growth.

Sometimes it is helpful to rely on a trusted and valued friend to help you recover from such a devastating loss.

NOTES

_____

_____

_____

_____

_____

GRIEF BRIEF 99

COMPLICATION

REJECTION

A child who suffers the loss of their parent may suffer feelings of abandonment. In some instances, true abandonment is experienced. These feelings and realities are horrendous to suffer.

If you know a child who has lost a parent and you are able to step forward, realize that you will never replace that parent in the child's mind.

Agree with yourself that the help and assistance you render is reward enough.

The child may even express resentment toward the kind soul rendering their emotional assistance and physical support.

These are natural emotions and you should not accept them as a reflection upon your efforts.

Realize that the child's emotions are a rejection of their parent's death, rather than of you and your efforts.

In my opinion, every young child suffering the loss of one or both parents should have supervised professional counseling.

Parental loss is devastating, spiritually damaging, and should be taken seriously.

NOTES

GRIEF BRIEF 100
COMPLICATION
EXCLUSION

When one is in love one does not expect to lose the object of their affection.

Problems arise within the family structure when a marriage contract is not in place.

A boyfriend, girlfriend, or fiancé may find that they are neither considered nor included in the family grief circle.

This lack of consideration presents certain difficulties for the disregarded survivor.

Grief may even be exacerbated by this exclusion or indifference.

This situation may increase the possibilities of complicated grief for the survivor.

It may be necessary for the unrecognized survivor to seek other ways to resolve their grief.

NOTES

_____

_____

_____

_____

_____

www.MourningCoffee.com

(903) 796-9669

101

www.MourningCoffee.com
(903) 796-9669

ABOUT THE AUTHOR

www.MourningCoffee.com

(903) 796-9669

ABOUT THE AUTHOR

My name is Tracy Renee Lee. I am a Certified Grief Counselor (GC-C), Managing Funeral Director (FDIC), and owner of Queen City Funeral Home in Queen City, Texas. I am an author and syndicated columnist. I write books, weekly bereavement articles, and grief briefs related to understanding and coping with grief. I am the American Funeral Director of the Year Runner-Up, recipient of the BBB's Integrity award, and co-founder of Heaven Sent, Corp and The Michael Joseph Arnot Memorial.

I deliver powerful messages and motivate survivors toward positive recovery.

It is my life's work to comfort the bereaved and help them live on.

For additional encouragement, read other articles or watch video "Grief Briefs," please go to my website at www.MourningCoffee.com.

A TRIBUTE TO MY DEAR FRIEND

PRESTON MC CONKIE
October 13, 1968 – December 11, 2012

PRESTON MC CONKIE

October 13, 1968 – December 11, 2012

THANKSGIVING

I had a dear friend die this past year. Although he passed away in a different state, I go to his social media page and leave him messages every now and then. I miss him so terribly, because he was an amazing human being. His heart was true and good, and he was honest with his fellow man and with himself. He was a friend to my family, and when you met him, you loved him, because of his goodness. My friend died smack dab in the middle of Thanksgiving and Christmas. How like him, he died in the season of family tradition and giving, two things he revered.

It would be easy to be miserable this year, thinking of how much we miss our dear friend, but he would not want that. Instead, we will remember all of the good that he contributed during his short life. We will be thankful for the time we had with him, the growth he inspired in us, his kindness, his generosity and for his passion for truth.

I read his obituary today, for the first time. It spoke volumes about my friend. It mentioned his accomplishments, which were many; and then, there was a paragraph that told who he was. *"Preston always stood up for correct principals. He was a scriptorian, loved music, upheld the Constitution, big on self-sufficiency and was courageous and undaunted." (Richfield Reaper, December 2012)* I am thankful for so many things, and although I may shed a tear that he is gone, I will forever remain grateful for the influence of my dear friend, and the example he set for me.

The holidays can be a very difficult time for someone who has lost a loved one, especially if this is his or her first holiday season since the loss. Even though we try to focus on how much better our lives are for having had our loved one, we miss them so terribly, that it is difficult to experience the cheer of the season.

If you know someone suffering through his or her first holiday season after loss, please be mindful of him or her. This is a particularly difficult time and they may feel lonely and isolated. Take a moment to remember with them, the wonderful moments of life they shared with their loved one. Participate in family traditions and create new ones that honor their deceased. Your blessings will be great, and you will have helped someone through a time, when your good acts of kindness were priceless.

That is what my friend Preston would have done.

(Mourning Coffee for the Mourning Soul I 2014, Tracy Renee Lee)

Preston's Humor

Too Few

I rose from my bed early this morning, suffering from a night of poor rest, due to uncomfortable rumblings in my tummy. I went to my recliner. Not wishing to disturb my husband's sleep with the noise of the television, I grabbed my iPad and began searching the internet.

It is interesting how early morning reflections take your mind to places you do not expect. This morning, my mind wandered as my fingers typed, and I found myself at a friend's blog. His last entry was November 11, 2012. He died just 30 days later, December 11, 2013. I read his writings, and as I did, I began to miss my friend, profoundly. Preston was such an honest person; his whole life was transparent and literally an open book. He was a writer, and I find evidence of his incredible talent all over the internet. His blog is filled with his personal thoughts and experiences, and reading it brought stinging tears to my eyes and a deep ache to my heart.

I miss my friend so deeply, and I wish I had known he was going to die prematurely. The truth of life, however, is that we do not know when our loved ones will die. We simply live our lives until we, or they, are gone. The secret of life is living it as though every moment might be your last. Do not waste your time counting moments and accomplishments. Make your moments count by molding this world into something better for those whom you leave behind. That is how my friend Preston lived his life.

Preston was a Gulf War Veteran, newspaper editor, novelist, Wikipedia contributor, and literary mentor. He was kind, respectful and honest, but most of all, Preston was a friend that inspired others to achieve better than their best. He was bold and would fight the good fight for those who were weaker than he, and he did it because it was the right thing to do, rather than for personal gain.

Through the years, as Preston called and visited, I would tell him of my admiration, my appreciation and my love for him. Now that he is gone, I long for one more conversation. I yearn to be able to say, "Preston, I cherish the blessing that brought you into my life."

The world has too few Prestons.

(Too Few, Mourning Coffee for the Mourning Soul II, Tracy Renee Lee, 2015)

Preston the Pirate

Preston had a brain tumor. Just before his death, he endured surgery to remove it. The surgery was a success, but Preston died within a year from a blood clot to his heart. Before his surgery, the tumor began affecting his eye control. He wore this eye patch to conceal it. True to his humor, Preston played it to the nines.

www.MourningCoffee.com

(903) 796-9669

SOAP

Isn't it funny, how a simple moment can bring forward in one's mind, sweet memories of a departed loved one?

This morning as I prepared for my shower, I realized for the third day in a row, that my soap bar was now a mere sliver and completely incapable of fulfilling its purpose of providing me with ample lather to clean and refresh my body for the day's events. Fortunately, I had not yet stepped into my shower, so I walked over to my lavatory and being unable to bend due to back issues, I reached into the cabinet beneath it, blindly searching for a fresh bar of soap. As I grabbed hold of the soap, neatly wrapped in lightly colored paper, my mind reflected back to a friend of mine, who each Christmas would send me a year supply of his homemade soap.

Preston's soap was never neatly wrapped in lightly colored paper, nor was it perfectly formed into smooth ergonomic shapes. His soap was made from the finest ingredients, engineered for sensitive skin and cut into simple squares. Preston shared his wonderful soap with those he loved and cared for most in the world.

My friend Preston was so dear to me. His love of Christ and his redeeming mission was so strong. From the first time I met Preston, he always sought to share his testimony with those who were searching for meaning in life.

As I rose and prepared for my shower this morning, Preston was not on my mind. Blindly reaching under the lavatory for a bar of soap, made me miss him so deeply. I was touched by the imagery of blindly searching for soap, to those who labor in search of their purpose.

GRIEF FACT 149

YANKED

Grief is all-consuming, it is no respecter of persons or time. You may have several weeks of great recovery and suddenly find yourself in the pitfalls of despair. This is a normal response.

Eventually, despair and loneliness will be replaced with kind and fond memories. Even so, you will be yanked back from time to time by the least little insignificant thing.

(Tracy Renee Lee, Mourning Glory II)

I smiled as I cried, remembering Preston's kind spirit and his willingness to share it with everyone he knew. I thought to myself, how appropriate it was, that this Easter morning, an insignificant sliver of soap, yanked my memories back to Preston and his willingness to share his testimony of Christ and his redeeming mission.

This morning I miss my dear friend, I miss his wonderful soap that he so thoughtfully sent me every year, and I miss his amazing testimony of Christ. This Easter morning as I prepared for my shower, I realized my day would be filled with thanksgiving for Christ's redeeming sacrifice, along with fond memories of my dear friend's willingness to share his Savior's message.

My day was bittersweet.

(Soap, Mourning Coffee for the Mourning Soul III, Tracy Renee Lee, 2016)

Preston's Amazing Soap

www.MourningCoffee.com

(903) 796-9669

DON PRESTON MCCONKIE, 44, PASSED AWAY DEC. 11, 2012, IN WASHINGTON CITY.

He was born Oct. 13, 1968, in Vernal, to Charles Collier and Geraldine Caldwell McConkie.

Preston grew up in Central Valley, where he attended local schools.

He joined the U.S. Army in 1987 through 1991, stationed in Korea, participated in Desert Shield and Desert Storm.

He served in the England Preston Mission, taught LDS seminary in Arizona, newspaper reporter and editor in Utah and Arizona. He was a long-haul truck driver for many years.

Preston always stood up for correct principals. He was a scriptorian, loved music, upheld the Constitution, big on self-sufficiency and was courageous and undaunted.

Survived by children, Carver, Janet Lee and Rebecca; mother, Geraldine "Deena" (Ron) Hawley; siblings, Charlotte (Keith) Williams, James Anthon (Sally) Burningham, Shara Dean (James) Mitchell, Eli Andrew (Katie) Burningham and Gina Petrice (Caleb) Rose. Preceded in death by father.

Funeral services took place Dec. 14 in the Annabella LDS ward chapel, with Bishop Louis Brown officiating.

Compassionate services were provided by the Annabella LDS 1st ward Relief Society.

A family prayer was shared by James Burningham (brother), and the invocation was given by James Mitchell (brother-in-law).

The organist was Earlene Larsen.

Musical selections included "The Lord Is My Shepherd," performed by the Williams family; a selection by Janet McConkie (daughter); and "Be Still, My Soul," an organ solo performed by Earlene Larsen.

Tributes were given by Shara Mitchell (sister), Story Mendez (niece) and Caleb Rose (brother-in-law), with a poem read by Caleb Rose. Janet Mathie (grandmother) introduced the children, and remarks were shared by Louis Brown.

The benediction was offered by Eli Burningham (brother).

Pallbearers included Carver McConkie, Eli Burningham, James Burningham, Keith Williams, Ben Williams, Chad Williams, James Mitchell, Alex Mitchell, Parker Mitchell, Braden Mitchell, Caleb Rose, Dean Roundy and Brooks Briggs.

Interment was in the Annabella Cemetery with military rites accorded by the VFW Sevier Post #5050 and Utah Honor Guard.

The dedicatory prayer was provided by Ron Hawley (step father).

www.MourningCoffee.com

(903) 796-9669

For your convenience,
Grief BRIEFs
may be found in
video format at
www.MourningCoffee.com.

Additionally,
Bereavement Articles and
Ask a Director
may be found there as well.

ADDITIONAL BOOKS
WRITTEN BY TRACY RENEÉ LEE

MOURNING LIGHT II
An additional 100 Facts,
Strategies & Wisdom
to help survivors
cope & recover
from the darkest
depths of grief.

MOURNING COFFEE
FOR THE MOURNING SOUL
A series of books
containing true bereavement stories
as experienced by funeral director
Tracy Reneé Lee.

SAYING GOODBYE
Children and adult coloring books
that introduce and help survivors
understand and cope with the experience of death.
It introduces and explains the unfamiliar things one will see
and experience before, during, and after a death and the accompanying services.

www.MourningCoffee.com

(903) 796-9669

SOMEONE HAS DIED

A series of illustrated children's books
designed to assist adults introduce and explain
the event of death,
the accompanying services during funeral week,
and appropriate behavior for children attending services.
"I wrote these two books to help quell a child's fear of death
and to create a safer environment for them while at the funeral home."
(Tracy Reneé Lee)
These stories are told through the lives of furry friends Lady
and Butter, service dogs at Queen City Funeral Home..

MOURNING LIGHT FOR CHILDREN

A unique coloring book for children,
containing 200 Grief BRIEFs,
written in language geared at a child's comprehension level.
This book will assist children in
understanding,
traversing,
and recovering
from the grief experience.

PURCHASE ADDITIONAL BOOKS AT

www.Amazon.com

or

www.Barnes&Noble.com

or

Barnes & Noble Order Desk

www.MourningCoffee.com
(903) 796-9669

127

23770471R00078

Made in the USA
Columbia, SC
15 August 2018